D0604155

DATE DUE

			MAR 04
MAY 28 04			
OCT 27 06			
209			
GAYLORD			PRINTED IN U.S.A.

Health Matters
Food and Your Health

by Jillian Powell

RSVP

RAINTREE
STECK-VAUGHN
PUBLISHERS
The Steck-Vaughn Company

Titles in the series

Drugs and Your Health
Exercise and Your Health
Food and Your Health
Hygiene and Your Health

Published by Raintree Steck-Vaughn Publishers, an imprint of Steck-Vaughn Company

Library of Congress Cataloging-in-Publication Data
Powell, Jillian.
Food and Your Health / Jillian Powell.
    p.   cm.—(Health Matters)
    Includes bibliographical references and index.
    Summary: Provides an introduction to basic nutrition and the relationship between food and health.
    ISBN 0-8172-4925-7
    1. Nutrition—Juvenile literature.
    2. Food—Juvenile literature.
    [1. Nutrition. 2. Food.]
    I. Title. II. Series: Health matters.
    RA784.P684   1998
    613.2—dc21   97-3259

Printed in Italy. Bound in the United States.
1 2 3 4 5 6 7 8 9 0 02 01 00 99 98

Picture acknowledgments
Cephas 5, 13 both, 18; Chapel Studios 19, 25 top, 26; Greg Evans 15, 23, 25 bottom; Impact 29 (Roger Scruton); J. Allan Cash 7, 17, 24; Tony Stone 10 (Gray Mortimore), 12 (Steve Outram); Wayland Picture Library 4, 6, 9, 11, 14, 16, 20, 21, 22, 27, 28.

Contents

Food and Your Body

Your body is made up of the food you eat. You need lots of different kinds of food to stay healthy. We call this having a balanced diet. Everything you eat and drink is part of your diet.

Proteins are the body builders— bones, muscles, skin, hair, and tissues.

Different foods contain different nutrients that help the body work properly. Protein is used to build and repair your body. Carbohydrates give you energy. Fats keep you warm and can be stored in the body for energy. Vitamins and minerals help keep you healthy.

Carbohydrates are a good source of energy.

Vitamin A is good for your eyes, bones, and teeth.

Vitamin C keeps your bones and skin healthy and fights illness.

Iron keeps your blood healthy.

Fats help keep you warm and can be stored in the body for energy.

Calcium keeps your bones and teeth strong.

These are the main types of foods you need.

FATS

PROTEINS

CARBOHYDRATES

VITAMINS & MINERALS

Eating a healthy diet helps keep your body fit and gives you lots of energy.

Cut out pictures of different types of food from newspapers and magazines. Stick them onto cardboard to make a collage, dividing them into the different types of nutrients. Think about the food you eat in one meal. Which groups do these fall into?

Food and Digestion

When you eat, your body breaks down the food so it can use the parts it needs. This is called digestion. First you bite into food and chew it with your teeth. The food mixes with saliva in your mouth. This softens it and starts to break it down.

You swallow the food, and muscles push it down a long tube into your stomach. There it mixes with juices that break it down. The mashed-up food moves into the small intestine and mixes with more juices. The nutrients then pass into the blood or go to the liver to be stored. Waste parts go into the large intestine where water is squeezed out. You get rid of the waste when you go to the toilet.

Chewing is the first part of digestion. Food is softened by chewing and saliva.

Left: Your body is about 66 percent water.

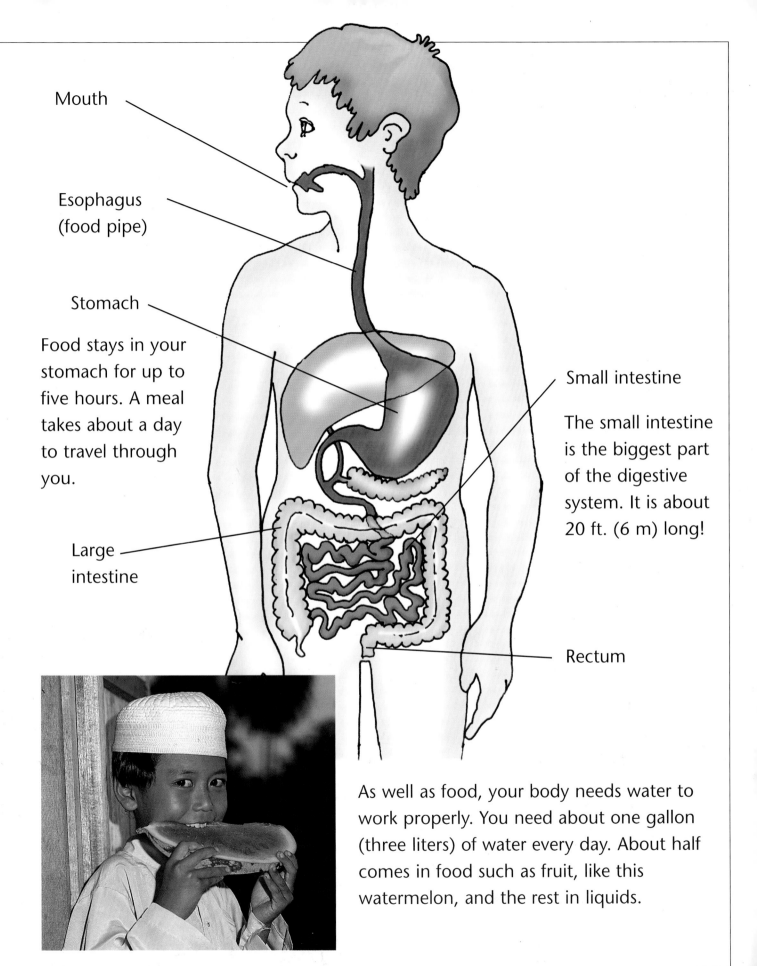

Mouth

Esophagus
(food pipe)

Stomach

Food stays in your
stomach for up to
five hours. A meal
takes about a day
to travel through
you.

Large
intestine

Small intestine

The small intestine
is the biggest part
of the digestive
system. It is about
20 ft. (6 m) long!

Rectum

As well as food, your body needs water to
work properly. You need about one gallon
(three liters) of water every day. About half
comes in food such as fruit, like this
watermelon, and the rest in liquids.

Food for Growing

Your body is made up of millions of tiny parts called cells. Until you are about 18 years old, your body makes new cells in order to grow. It also needs to repair and replace old cells all your life. The energy to make and repair body cells comes from your food. Body-building foods contain protein.

Your body is made up of cells, which are repaired and replaced throughout your life.

Bone cell

Protein comes from animals and plants. Foods that contain lots of protein include meat, fish, eggs, cheese, milk, nuts, and pulses. When you digest your food, proteins are broken down so they can be used to build different body parts like muscles, hair, skin, and blood cells.

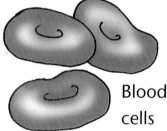

Blood cells

Nerve cell

Muscle cells

Protein helps build muscle. There are about 650 muscles in your body. Almost half your weight is muscle!

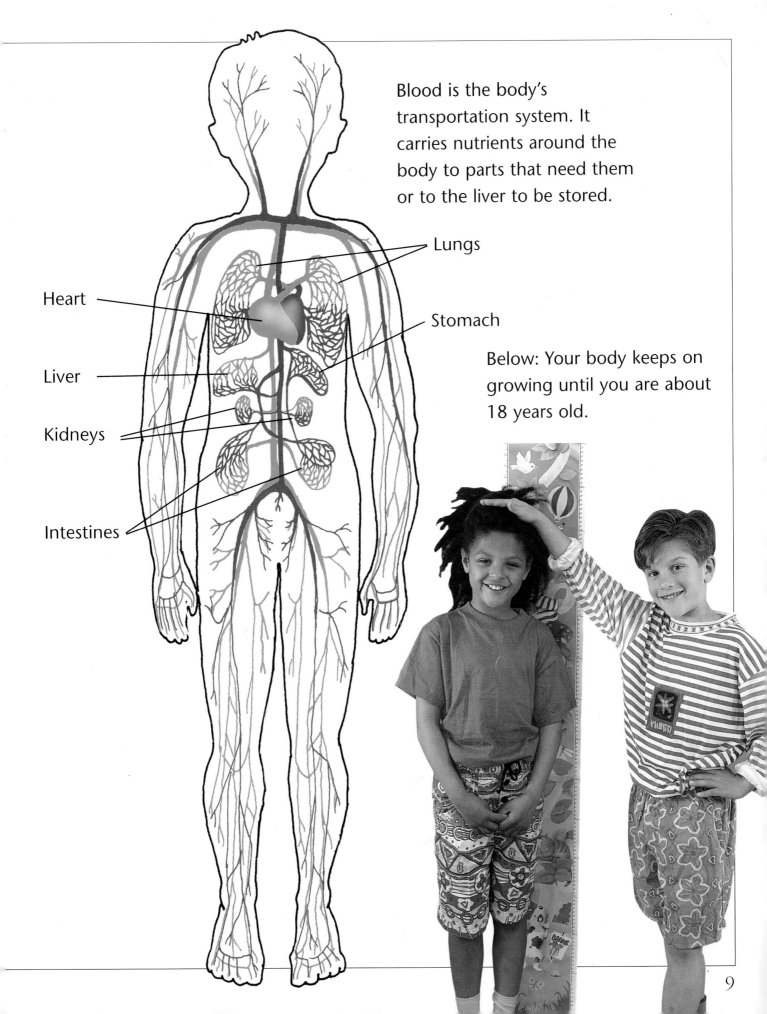

Blood is the body's transportation system. It carries nutrients around the body to parts that need them or to the liver to be stored.

Lungs

Heart

Stomach

Liver

Below: Your body keeps on growing until you are about 18 years old.

Kidneys

Intestines

Food for Energy

Food gives your body energy. Your body needs energy to grow, to repair itself, and to stay active.

Foods that give your body lots of energy are starchy carbohydrates like pasta, bread, cereals, rice, and potatoes. They also contain some protein, vitamins, and minerals. About a third of all the food you eat should be starchy carbohydrates. They should be the main part of each meal.

People who play sports eat lots of starchy foods to give them energy.

Energy in food and drink is measured in calories.
(1 calorie is the amount of energy needed to raise the
heat of 1 kg of water by one degree centigrade)
A glass of milk containing 100 calories will give you
enough energy to dance for ten minutes or watch
television for 1¹/₄ hours.

These foods contain 100 calories

| 2 slices of bread | 1 banana | 7–8 nuts | 1¹/₂ apples |

Carbohydrates
are found in
foods like
potatoes.

**As children grow, they need
approximately the following
number of calories
per day:**

Boys
2,400–2,800

Girls
2, 200–2,400

Boys need
more energy
because they are generally
bigger than girls.

Fats in Food

You need some types of fat to keep you healthy, but many people eat too much fat. Fatty foods can make you overweight and keep your heart from working properly.

Some fats are easy to see, like fat on meat, fried foods, and cream. Others are hidden in foods like cakes, cookies, sausages, ice cream, and nuts. Fats keep the body warm and give you energy. The fat in oily fish like sardines and tuna can help the blood flow around the body. But the fats found in meat and dairy foods can make the blood too sticky and cause heart disease.

Types of Fats
SATURATED
Milk
Cream
Butter
Coconut oil
Bacon

UNSATURATED
(poly and mono)
Olive oil
Sunflower oil
Grapeseed oil
Soya oil
Fish oil

There are types of fats, called saturates, monounsaturates, and polyunsaturates. For a healthy heart, cut back on saturates like animal fats.

Oily fish are a healthy source of unsaturated fats.

Cutting Down on Fat

Baked potatoes rather than French fries

Fat per 3.5 oz. (100 g)

Baked potatoes	0.2 g
French fries	6.7 g

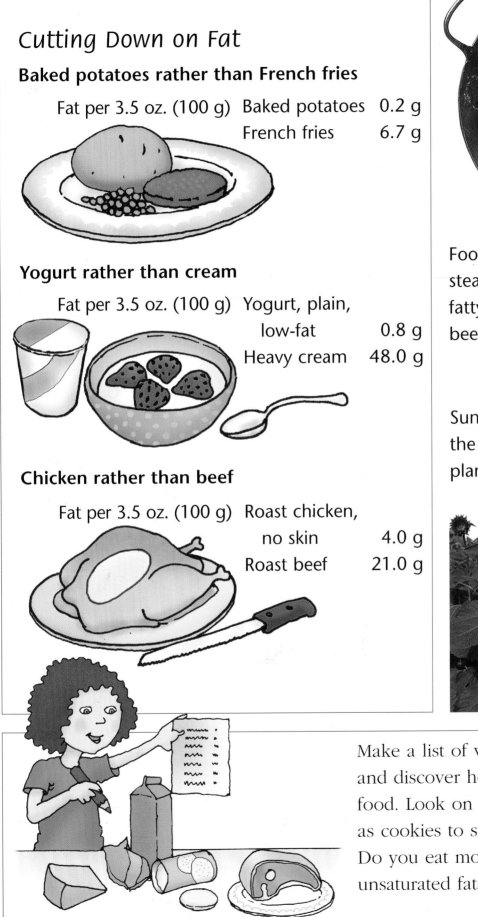

Yogurt rather than cream

Fat per 3.5 oz. (100 g)

Yogurt, plain, low-fat	0.8 g
Heavy cream	48.0 g

Chicken rather than beef

Fat per 3.5 oz. (100 g)

Roast chicken, no skin	4.0 g
Roast beef	21.0 g

Food that has been grilled, steamed, or stir-fried is less fatty than food that has been fried or roasted in fat.

Sunflower oil comes from the seeds of the sunflower plant.

Make a list of what you eat each day, and discover how much fat is in your food. Look on labels of foods such as cookies to see if they contain fats. Do you eat more saturated or unsaturated fats?

Food and Body Weight

You need to eat enough food to be the right weight for your height. If you eat more than you need, the extra food is stored as fat. If you don't eat enough food, your body can't grow or repair itself properly and you may get sick. It is not healthy to be too fat or too thin. If you are overweight, you need to cut down the number of calories in your food and drink and get more exercise.

Starchy foods like pasta, potatoes, fresh fruit, and vegetables contain lots of goodness but they are not fattening. Fatty and sugary foods like fried foods, cakes, and cookies contain more calories, so they can make you put on weight.

Find out if you have a healthy weight for your height. It will change as you grow!

Left: Foods that are not converted to energy can turn to fat, which is stored under the skin all around the body.

Food Rules

- Eat regular meals
- Don't skip meals
- Eat lots of starchy foods like bread and pasta
- Eat plenty of fresh fruit and vegetables

Right: Eating too many foods that are high in fats and sugar can make you overweight.

This pie chart shows you how much to eat of each of these types of foods:

- Bread, cereals, and potatoes
- Meat, fish, and alternatives
- Fat and sugar
- Milk and dairy products
- Fruit and vegetables

Fiber in Food

Fiber is a part of food that cannot be digested. It passes through and helps push waste out of your body. After you have swallowed your food, it is squeezed along tubes inside you. You need to eat fiber to help the tubes squeeze properly.

Fiber comes from plant foods like cereals, vegetables, and fruits. We eat it in bread, pasta, rice, cereals, fruit, and vegetables. The fiber in fruit and vegetables, including peas and beans, can help the blood flow around the body properly.

Foods like wild rice and whole-grain rice contain much more fiber than white rice.

Foods with no fiber include
cheese, sugar, fish, meat, ice cream, eggs, oil, fruit drinks

High Fiber Foods (per 3.5 oz. [100 g])

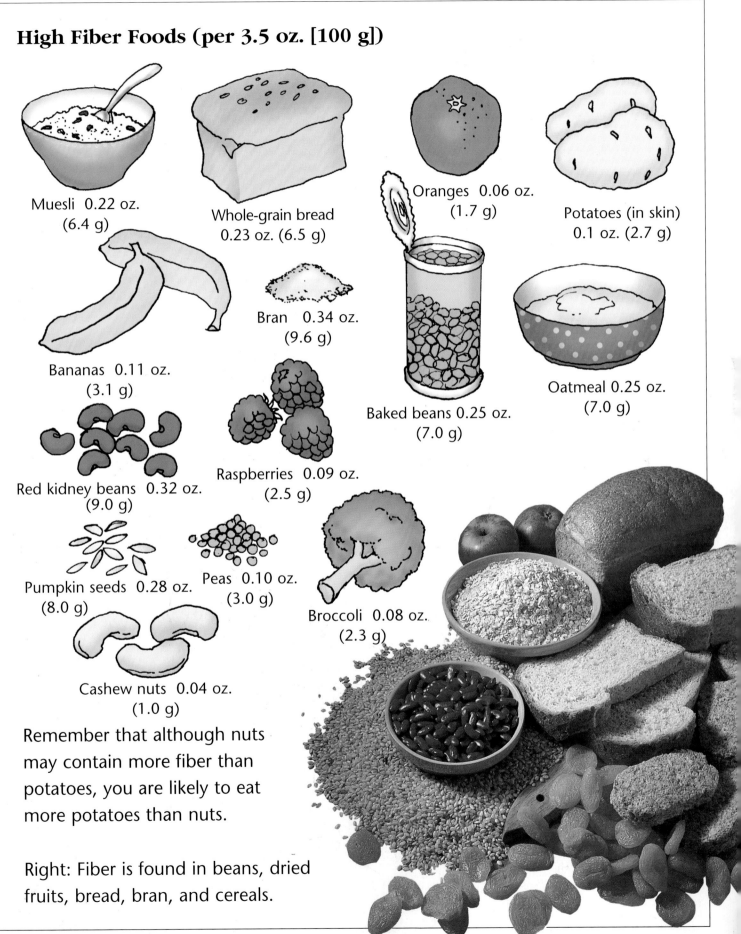

Muesli 0.22 oz. (6.4 g)

Whole-grain bread 0.23 oz. (6.5 g)

Oranges 0.06 oz. (1.7 g)

Potatoes (in skin) 0.1 oz. (2.7 g)

Bananas 0.11 oz. (3.1 g)

Bran 0.34 oz. (9.6 g)

Baked beans 0.25 oz. (7.0 g)

Oatmeal 0.25 oz. (7.0 g)

Red kidney beans 0.32 oz. (9.0 g)

Raspberries 0.09 oz. (2.5 g)

Pumpkin seeds 0.28 oz. (8.0 g)

Peas 0.10 oz. (3.0 g)

Broccoli 0.08 oz. (2.3 g)

Cashew nuts 0.04 oz. (1.0 g)

Remember that although nuts may contain more fiber than potatoes, you are likely to eat more potatoes than nuts.

Right: Fiber is found in beans, dried fruits, bread, bran, and cereals.

Vitamins and Minerals

Eating lots of different foods gives you the vitamins and minerals you need to stay healthy. Vitamins and minerals all help different parts of the body.

Vitamin C helps keep teeth, gums, and bones healthy and helps you fight colds. Vitamin K helps scars heal. The mineral calcium makes strong teeth and bones, and iron makes healthy red blood cells.

We only need tiny amounts of vitamins and minerals, but if we do not have enough, the body cannot work properly.

Fresh fruit and vegetables contain lots of vitamins and minerals. About a third of all the food you eat should be fruit and vegetables. Raw fruit and vegetables contain the most vitamins.

Some important vitamins and minerals and foods in which they are found.

Vitamin A
butter, eggs, carrots

Vitamin B1
cereals, milk, bread, meat, vegetables

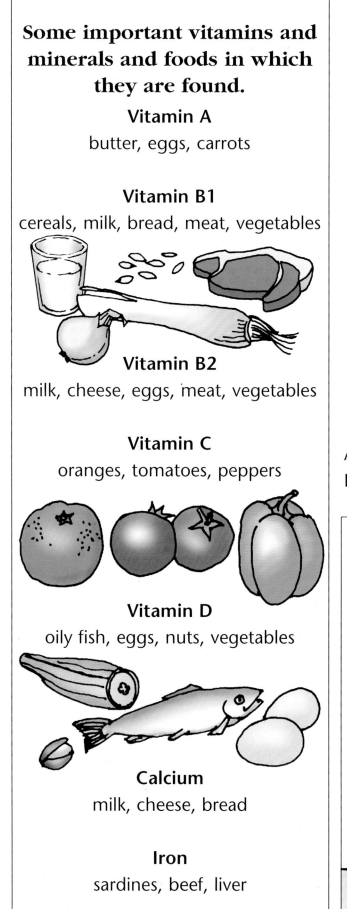

Vitamin B2
milk, cheese, eggs, meat, vegetables

Vitamin C
oranges, tomatoes, peppers

Vitamin D
oily fish, eggs, nuts, vegetables

Calcium
milk, cheese, bread

Iron
sardines, beef, liver

A glass of milk is a good source of calcium. It also contains vitamins A, B2, and D.

Salt is a mineral. We need about .10 oz. (3 g) of salt a day but most of us eat up to five times more! We add some salt to food but about two thirds comes in processed foods. Too much salt can lead to heart problems. Try not to add salt to food and cut down on salty foods like potato chips and bacon.

Food and Your Teeth

Eating too many sweet foods can ruin your teeth. Little scraps of food left in your mouth feed bacteria, which grow in warmth and moisture. Sugar makes bacteria grow fastest. The sugar and bacteria cover your teeth with a sticky coat called plaque.

Eating crunchy foods like apples and carrots helps keep your teeth clean and your gums healthy.

Plaque contains acids that can eat into the enamel on your teeth. If the acids make a hole, bacteria can get inside and rot the tooth, so it will need a filling. Brushing your teeth after meals helps keep plaque from forming.

The average person eats his or her own weight in sugar every year.

Candy contains lots of sugar, so always brush your teeth after eating it.

Tooth Rules

- brush your teeth at least twice daily
- change your toothbrush every two months
- use dental floss to clean between your teeth
- see the dentist twice a year

You know when you add sugar to food but did you know that foods like cakes and cookies, soups, sausages, and baked beans all contain sugar? Look on food cans, jars, and packages and make a list of all the foods that have sugar added. How much does each contain? Can you find any of the same sorts of food that have no added sugar?

Food Additives

A lot of the food we buy today comes ready for us to cook or eat. Additives are chemicals that are added to make food last longer, taste better, or look nicer.

Natural additives come from plants like beets, which gives a red color. Others are made with chemicals, like saccharin. This sweetens but has fewer calories than sugar. Preservatives help food last longer. Colorings add color. Flavorings make flavors stronger.

There are also additives that make foods smoother and creamier. They stop fats and water from separating in foods like ice cream and peanut butter.

Additives should be listed on the outside of all packaged foods.

These foods all contain additives

Ham, bacon, sausages

Pie fillings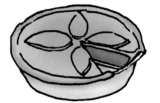

Packaged soups

Cookies

Sandwich spread

Drinks

Compare labels of the same foods that contain additives. Look carefully at the package to see what it contains compared with another brand.

Artificial color has been added to these candies.

Problem Foods

Some people cannot eat certain foods because they make them sick. This is called having a food allergy.

Foods like milk, eggs, bananas, oranges, and peanuts can make some people sick. Food additives can also make some people sick. Children can become hyperactive if they eat food colorings like Tartrazine and Sunset Yellow. People with diabetes must not eat too many sugary or sweet foods.

Some people cannot eat anything that contains wheat or wheat flour, such as cereals, bread, cakes, or cookies.

Some people cannot eat these foods because they are allergic to them:

shrimps

mussels

nuts
strawberries

milk
eggs
bananas

People who are allergic to wheat cannot eat bread made from wheat flour.

Some people don't eat meat because of their religion. Hindus and some Sikhs don't eat meat. Muslims and Jews don't eat pork.

Religion and Food

Hindus do not eat beef, because a cow is considered a holy animal.

Buddhists respect all living creatures, because they believe they have souls that will be reborn.

Sikhs do not eat beef, but it is not forbidden.

Muslims have "halal" (permitted) and "haram" (not permitted) foods. They do not eat pork or its products because it is thought to be "unclean."

Jews have laws that state whether food is clean or unclean. Sheep, cows, and goats are clean, but the pig is unclean. Some religions also have rules about how food should be prepared.

Additives can give you
Skin rashes
Stomach upsets
Breathing difficulties

Vegetarian food does not include meat. Vegetarians think it is wrong to kill animals for food, and they don't like the way animals are farmed. Some people think it is more healthy to eat a vegetarian diet.

Food Safety

The food we eat must be fresh and clean, or it can make us sick. Bacteria need warmth and moisture to grow, so keeping food cold in a refrigerator or frozen can help make it last longer. Bacteria from raw foods, especially meat, can spread to cooked foods, so they must be kept apart.

Bacteria are tiny living things. Thousands could fit onto a pinhead. If we eat food that has bacteria on it, it can make us sick.

Foods like fruit and salads should be washed before we eat them to get rid of any germs and chemical sprays. Cooked foods, especially poultry and pork, must be thoroughly cooked to kill any bacteria that could make us ill. If food has been frozen, it must be properly defrosted before it is cooked, or it may not get cooked through.

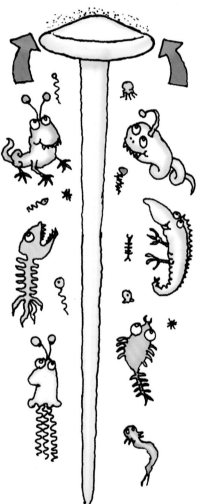

Left: Wash vegetables thoroughly, because they may still contain chemicals.

Food spoils when bacteria start growing on it. Bacteria can make bread and fruit turn moldy and milk and cream turn sour.

Food Safety Rules

- Always wash hands before touching food
- Keep everything in the kitchen clean
- Don't cough or sneeze over food
- Keep pets, flies, and mice away from food

Collect labels from processed foods like yogurts, cans, and frozen and chilled foods. What are the storage instructions? Which last the longest? Which last the shortest time? Make a chart showing how different types of food should be stored.

Healthy Food

Having a healthy, balanced diet means eating lots of different foods that give your body the nutrients it needs. Health foods include natural foods like whole-meal bread and whole-grain rice, beans, and lentils. They contain important nutrients like carbohydrates and vitamins but no added sugar, salt, or additives. Organic food is food farmed without using chemicals.

Unhealthy foods are candy, cakes, cookies, and soft drinks. They contain lots of sugar, fat, and additives and no important nutrients. It is best to eat them only as snacks now and then.

Ice creams are eaten as treats now and then.

A Balanced Diet
There are five main food groups.

1. Starchy foods like cereals, potatoes, pasta, rice

2. Dairy foods like milk, butter, cheese

5. Fatty and sugary foods like cake

3. Fruit and vegetables

4. Meat, poultry, fish

A balanced meal contains food from each of the first four groups. Group five foods should only be eaten as snacks from time to time.

Some people prefer to buy food that has been produced at an organic farm.

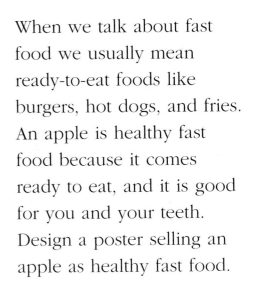

When we talk about fast food we usually mean ready-to-eat foods like burgers, hot dogs, and fries. An apple is healthy fast food because it comes ready to eat, and it is good for you and your teeth. Design a poster selling an apple as healthy fast food.

Glossary

Bacteria Tiny living things. Some can be harmful but others are helpful.

Calories How we measure energy in food.

Carbohydrate A part of food that gives us energy.

Defrosted Thawed so no ice is left.

Diabetes A disease that means the body can't control the amount of sugar glucose in the blood.

Digestion What the body does to break down food and use nutrients.

Fat A part of food that keeps us warm and gives energy.

Food allergy When people cannot eat certain foods because the foods make them sick.

Hyperactive Overenergetic.

Nutrients Goodness in food that the body can use.

Protein A part of food that we need to grow and repair body cells.

Vegetarian Someone who does not eat meat.

Vitamins and Minerals Nutrients found in food that we need to keep us healthy.

Whole-meal and whole-grain Cereals that have the whole grain and have not had any part taken away.

Books to Read

Parker, Steve. *Food & Digestion*. (Human Body.) Danbury, CT: Franklin Watts, 1990.

Ballard, Carol. *The Stomach & Digestive System*. (Human Body.) Austin, TX: Raintree Steck-Vaughn, 1997.

Ganeri, Anita. *What's Inside Us?* (How Do We Know.) Austin, TX: Raintree Steck-Vaughn, 1995.

Figtree, Dale. *Eat Smart: A Guide to Good Health for Kids*. Clinton, NJ: New Win Publishing, 1992.

Patent, Dorothy H. *Nutrition*. (What's in the Food We Eat.) New York: Holiday House, 1992.

Index